An Immigrant

Orphan Goes to War

The Civil War Experience of August Ganske

Benjamin T. Phelps

In memory of my grandmother

Virginia "Ginny" Steinhorst Phelps (1923-2015)

Contents

Introduction	4
Early Life	7
War Clouds	11
Camp Randall	16
Away to Dixie	24
White River Expedition	38
The Angel of Wisconsin	44
Never Forgotten	53
Bibliography	57
Endnotes	58

Introduction

This short book is about the life and Civil War experiences of my great-great-great-grandfather, August Ganske. The last living link in my line of his descendants, my great-grandmother Cora Ganske Steinhorst, died before I reached one and a half years. Since my family's collective memory on August Ganske was nearly non-existent, I endeavored to learn as much as I could about my ancestor and his service in the 29th Wisconsin Infantry Regiment during the Civil War by conducting primary source research and by reaching out to distant relatives. I am particularly thankful to Don Ganske, Julia Woodward, and Chad Ganske.

Ganske certainly risked everything and nearly lost his life before he married and had any children. While he was only on active duty in enemy territory for half of November 1862, his regiment was called into battle formation more than once. Ganske participated on the First White River Expedition; an aborted operation conducted by the Army of the Southwest early in Ulysses S. Grant's Vicksburg Campaign. Ganske's unit, the 29th Wisconsin Regiment of Volunteers, suffered only one casualty from enemy fire during this time. However, there were many other dangers.

Disease caused more disability and death in the Civil War than combat.[1] Ganske was one of these victims.

      Ganske seems to have seen his service in the Union army as unavoidable but would later reflect with pride on his relatively short period of service. While it is clear that Ganske suffered from the horrors of war, it is quite possible that he inflicted them as well. The 29th Wisconsin was in Confederate territory less than 24 hours before it engaged in a massive raid, called "foraging," on local civilians. It is uncertain if Ganske participated in this raid but considering how the regiment continued to regularly "forage" from its camp and often rotated its troops through various duties, it is very likely he participated in foraging parties. While foraging had always been part of warfare and Union troops nominally raided only from confirmed secessionists and rebels, many lamented that Union soldiers and their officers commonly made no distinction between Southerners, even targeting the elderly, widows, and the enslaved. Many of Ganske's contemporaries in the 29th Wisconsin wrote home disapproving of such practices and would often call out other Union regiments for their unruly and unscrupulous behavior.

Yet the Union presence also provided concrete opportunities for the enslaved to liberate themselves and find refuge in Union camps. Ganske's contemporaries also left a wide variety of anti-slavery and pro-emancipation opinions.

Unfortunately, there are no extant letters, diaries, or accounts from Ganske relating to his Civil War experience apart from some nearly illegible papers filed with his pension applications and some recollections recorded by one of his granddaughters. Nevertheless, records from the National Archives copied by Don Ganske, provide an accurate outline of Ganske's Civil War service in the 29th Wisconsin. Using the dates given in the documents, it is possible to reconstruct Ganske's general experiences through the personal and official accounts from his regiment. While Ganske's thoughts and views are unknown, I purposely included various points of view to demonstrate what his fellow soldiers experienced and thought.

Early Life

August Martin Ganske was born to Mr. and Mrs. Martin Ganske on September 9, 1833 in Ludwigsdorf in the Province of Posen in the Kingdom of Prussia, near the border with the Kingdom of Poland, part of the Russian Empire. Both of August's parents died when he was very young. When he was three August taken in by his uncle Stephan Ganske. Uncle Stephan saw to August's education and saw to it that August was confirmed in the Lutheran Church. Sadly, August's "good aunt" died, and Stephan remarried. Unfortunately, "kind" Uncle Stephan died soon thereafter, and the "pleasant home" was "broken up."[2]

Approximate Location of Ludwigsdorf

This may not have been a case of a fairytale "wicked stepmother." Family laws in the 19th century incorporated the concept of *coverture* whereby, upon marriage, a woman's legal rights and obligations were subsumed by those of her husband. Furthermore, in some regions a widow would have to declare that she would never remarry if she wanted to retain guardianship of her own children.[3] It may have been more financially and legally practical for the widowed step-aunt to arrange for August to make his own life elsewhere. She likely needed to remarry to ensure his own economic security—caring for a barely-related teenage boy as her own son may have threatened her future.

The Bay and Harbor of New York by Samuel Waugh (1814–1885), depicting the castle in 1848

In 1856, at the age of 23, Ganske sailed from Hamburg to Castle Garden, New York with a family from Ludwigsdorf named Weckworth. The party travelled, likely via boat on the Great Lakes, to Watertown, Wisconsin. While the Weckworths settled in Minnesota, Ganske stayed in Dodge County. On November 1st he swore his intentions to become a citizen of the United States and "to renounce forever all allegiance and fidelity" to the King of Prussia. Ganske first lived in the town of Clyman to work on the railroad and as hired farm hand. During his first winter Ganske worked for Henry Glover in Minnesota Junction. He later went to the town of Trenton to work for "Father" Cady, earning $14 a month. The Cadys were "kind Christian people" who made Ganske feel like he was part of their family. It is likely that through these close

Ganske's naturalization declaration and signature

relationships Ganske forsook the Lutheranism of his youth and assimilated with his English-speaking neighbors by joining the Presbyterian church.

After many months of hard work and saving, the orphaned immigrant was able to buy 80 acres of undeveloped land north of Beaver Dam. He began clearing the virgin forest and built a log house which he immediately rented out. Turning a wild wood into land suitable for farming took a lot of work. He "grubbed out" trees and stumps, cleared away stones, and split rails for fencing. Ganske then bought another 40 acres. While Ganske was working to clear his homestead, he would have little income until the land could produce a crop. So, while improving his property, he lived with and worked for Zury Whiting. Ganske could be optimistic that very soon he would fulfill his own American dream.[4]

By the 1860s Wisconsin was one of the largest wheat-producing regions in the world.

War Clouds

In 1860 Wisconsin had only been a state for 12 years. Still, it could boast a population of three quarters of a million. Like Ganske, over 100,000, or 15%, had been born in the German states.[5] Most Wisconsinites, like Ganske, worked as farmers in the southern part of the state.[6]

1860 also saw the contentious election of Abraham Lincoln. Wisconsin, like most northern states, voted for Lincoln. However, the disgruntled southern states feared for their futures under a Republican president and began seceding. Following the firing on Fort Sumter in April 1861 Lincoln and the northern governors issued calls for volunteers to put down the rebellion. While the recruitment quotas were easily filled, they proved to be far too small. In July 1862 Lincoln called for 300,000 more troops.

German-born Governor Edward Salomon

By the month of August, it was clear that states would not be able to reach their individual goals. The Militia Act called up the militia for nine months of service to fill the gaps. Governor Edward Salomon was ordered to enroll all able-bodied men between 18 and 45. Salomon then appointed draft commissioners and surgeons for each county.[7]

    The state determined that over 4,000 volunteers were still needed. The German-born Salomon sought to spread the burden a draft would place on communities by making foreign born men eligible if they met the requirements of declaring intent for citizenship and having voted in elections. Furthermore, many towns offered bounties to encourage volunteer enlistments. The threatened draft may have been designed to bring forth enough volunteers to make the draft itself unnecessary.[8] The War Department's orders to Governor Salomon were printed in the press and many papers added their voices to the call for volunteers to enlist.[9] Pastors and other community leaders urged single men to volunteer, so married men and fathers would not be forced to leave their families behind. On the afternoon of Sunday, August 17th a "war meeting" was held in the town of Trenton. The townsmen voted

Ganske's enlistment paper

to pay a staggering bounty of $100 per volunteer from the town to fill their quota.[10]

Ganske decided it was better to leave his farm behind willingly as a volunteer rather than be forced to enlist. One evening he went to the creamery in Trenton, where many of his neighbors would all be gathered, stood up on his milk wagon and intently implored the other young men to volunteer saying, "Now men if we don't enlist sooner or later we will have to go."

On August 21 Ganske, Benjamin Cady, Henry Whiting, and the others from Trenton enlisted, after passing a rudimentary medical examination. Ganske's enlistment papers provide a brief physical description. The 26-year-old farmer had gray eyes, brown hair, a "fair complexion," and measured five feet, eight inches tall.

    The *Fox Lake Gazette* noted the activity in Trenton approvingly, in a brief article titled "Well done Trenton." The *Gazette* reported that 59 men, mostly farmers, enlisted at one time.[11] Ganske later recalled,

> We dropped the rake and the cradle and went to the Town House in Trenton enlisted in the 29th Regiment, Company H, Wisconsin. First we went to Waupun where we drilled for four weeks and then to Camp Randall, Madison, where we received our equipment as soldiers and continued the daily drill and discipline which was needed to train and prepare young soldiers for the campaign and field of battle.[12]

Similar scenes were repeated across Dodge, Jefferson, Dane, and Columbia counties. Henry Whipple recorded in his diary that he and the men who enlisted at

Waterloo formed company A. For several days they were drilled by a veteran in a pasture.[13]

Orphaned and unmarried, Ganske had no family to leave behind and was fortunate to have several friends from Trenton in his company. Yet it still must have grieved him to leave behind his home and friends like the Cadys and Whittings. Writing on his knee for want of a table or desk, another new recruit recalled his last night with his family before he left for Camp Randall in Madison.

> Our entire family, ten, were home, the family circle having never been broken. Sad were the countenances, and sadder the hearts as we thought of the morrow; it came and with it the trembling lip and throbbing heart, as we bid all good bye.[14]

As summer ended, hundreds of young men from cities, villages, and townships across south-central Wisconsin rode in wagons through the mud and rain to the capital. Some had good accommodations. The unit from Fox Lake stopped in Columbus at an inn called the Whitney House[15] In most towns the men received a warm welcome from patriotic citizens.

Camp Randall

I have heard of war, read of war, played war, but never before engaged in war.

—a recruit at Camp Randall, October 16, 1862.[16]

On September 27th the 29th Wisconsin Infantry Regiment officially completed its muster under Colonel Charles R. Gill. Gill, a lawyer, had been a state senator for two years before Governor Salomon appointed him to lead the new regiment. The state lacked men of military skill and experience to command regiments early in the war. The editor of the *Fox Lake Gazette* repeatedly complained that the 29th Wisconsin needed better, more qualified, officers.[17] While Gill may have been a politician officer, a writer for a Watertown paper believed that Gill was not a poor choice saying,

> While he does not pretend to any considerable knowledge or experience in military affairs, he at least stands on par in this respect with most if not all the new officers appointed since the war department refused to permit appoints from the army in the field…

Gill certainly showed early aptitude for leadership. Gill believed that Watertown had done too little in encouraging volunteer enlistments during the summer of 1862, so he initiated a war meeting in which he addressed "quite a large audience" with "earnestness and vehemence." One heckler called out that it was easy enough for Gill to encourage enlistments when he already had a commission and large pay. Gill then theatrically took his commission from his pocket, tore it up, and declared that he was ready to enlist as private for three years. Gill was almost certainly bluffing, but his words and actions had the desired effect. "His example was contagious and between forty and fifty came forward and enlisted at once." The company elected Gill captain and he was soon recommended for colonel, to which he was unsurprisingly "promoted." The other officers were a mixture of popular local men and experienced soldiers.[18]

Charles R. Gill

Many of Wisconsin's recruits went to Madison to be formally enlisted and formed into regiments. Camp Randall was established on the former state fairgrounds, covering 60 acres. An uneven high fence enclosed the camp and its parade ground in the center. Each company of the 29th Wisconsin was assigned a "street" in the camp and occupied the half of the two buildings facing it. Each building, designed for 40 men, was 50 feet long and 9 feet wide. The men slept in three tiers of bunkbeds upon issued straw and blankets—two men to a bunk. Despite the tight conditions one soldier noted his thankfulness for new buildings "free from vermin" and well-shingled roofs.[19]

Other soldiers of the 30th Wisconsin were quartered in the former stalls built against the unbattened fence. Despite being originally intended for animals, these new recruits found them to be adequate accommodations, one went as far as to call the fairgrounds-turned-barracks "wonderful." However, another soldier was less generous in his description

Camp Randall by John Gadis

saying that the barracks "are well calculated for astronomical observations."[20] Emilie Quiner, a 22-year-old woman living in Madison, often thought of the soldiers nearby. In her diary entry on October 2, 1862 she wrote: "How I pity the poor soldiers in camp. It is so cold and wet. I think they must suffer." Quiner and other women would attempt to improve the soldiers' morale by baking pies and delivering them to the camp.[21]

Otherwise, the soldiers' cooking and eating experience would vary depending on the weather since it was all done outdoors. The food rations primarily consisted of bread and beef or pork. The diet was supplemented by smaller amounts of potatoes, beans, rice, peas, sugar, and molasses as well as coffee and tea. In addition to foodstuffs, the infantrymen received weekly rations of soap, candles, and firewood.[22]

The recruit's time at Camp Randall was not very demanding. Soldiers likely found it more boring than fatiguing. One recruit described camp life,

> We drill 5 hours a day, the balance of the time is spent in reading, writing, sleeping, washing, mending, cooking, etc. It reminds me of a lumberman's life, which I have been used to, and I like it well. Some of the boys think it a little strange, but they will get used to it before long. They are patriotic boys and will make good soldiers.[23]

Others were forced to realize the differences between military and civilian life. One wrote,

> Our wills and wishes must subordinate themselves to others. But when we contemplate the end in view, being, as it is, nothing less than the ransom of our nation from anarchy and annihilation, the maintaining for those who shall come after us the blessings we inherited, we are satisfied to do and suffer all things—even to the loss of life itself.[24]

On October 15 the 29th Wisconsin finally received their uniforms. An eyewitness recruit of the 30th regiment described their appearance and activity. "They were dressed in light blue overcoats and pants, dark blue undercoats and black hats with a black feather on one side. The 29th was on battalion drill this morning and made a very fine appearance…"[25] The "splendid" Springfield rifle was their primary weapon.[26] Two weeks later the 30th regiment received their uniforms. This greatly excited some of the "boys" in the regiment. One soldier remarked, "some went strutting, putting on airs…others met and shook hands as if old friends had just met." With such a fine appearance, "who would not be a soldier?"[27] Many young men burst into "three cheers for the Union" or "Bully for Uncle Sam."

Men of the 2nd Wisconsin Infantry wearing uniforms like those later issued to the 29th Wisconsin

Yet this cheerfulness was juxtaposed with "sober hours" and "times of reflection."[28] After a year of bloody battles at Shiloh, the Peninsula, Antietam, and elsewhere, the soldiers must have considered the distinct possibilities of their own violent deaths. This would certainly be difficult to put out of mind when newsboys would "pop in…crying at the top of his voice 'another great battle,'" Yet the possibility of a non-violent, but nonetheless wretched death from disease was even greater. Many soldiers became sick in the close living conditions of the camp. While most suffered

21

only from colds, at least one soldier from the 29th Wisconsin died from disease in October.[29]

Many of the young men had likely never stayed away from home and family and wrestled with homesickness. At the end of October relatives of soldiers in the 29th Wisconsin visited their sons, brothers, husbands, and fathers in camp. They brought with them "the common luxuries of home, as a remembrance." They spoke "words of cheer," offered advice and received final instructions on how to carry on life and business during their soldier's absence. When it was time for the visitors to depart, the soldier would escort his loved ones to the gate to say the final goodbyes. One soldier described the dejected emotions,

> they pass along, and he looks so steady, so sober, but his eyes begin to glisten as he turns away with a heart to a full, a throat choked for utterance, perhaps it is the last good bye, to the dearest of earth; and we instantly turn our thoughts homeward and ask, how many of us for the last time, have bidden our dearest ones, those precious words, *good bye*.[30]

Already in Camp Randall the soldiers began to rely on letters to combat homesickness and loneliness. "O how anxiously we look for letters, and the boys literally dance for joy when they receive one." The soldiers were often prolific letter-writers and had plenty of time to spend writing, if not ideal circumstances. Gathering around the fires, soldiers would write letters, using planks and boxes as desks, "with eyes nearly blinded with smoke." Others sat in their bunks "writing and shivering."[31] If Ganske wrote letters, sadly none survive. Although he had no immediate family, he had close friends and neighbors; perhaps he had already begun courting his future wife, Margaret Anna Krause of Clyman.

Another view of Camp Randall. Note the proximity to rail service.

Away to Dixie

On Friday, October 31st, Governor Edward Salomon addressed the 29th Wisconsin, standing in formation, from horseback. According to one eyewitness, he offered an "encouraging and complimentary speech" and referenced the praise that General George McClellan had given to the Wisconsin units fighting in the east. At the end, the regiment gave "three hearty cheers" for the governor followed by three more each for the Union and the colonel. Then former governor Randall stood up in his buggy and offered an "eloquent" speech in which he commended the men for their physical strength and bravery while urging them to restrain themselves from laying "rude hands on defenseless women and children, but whenever they met a rebel to smite him, and wherever it was expedient to leave a spectacle of rebel on a tree." This speech too received "three lusty cheers." Then the men of the 29th Wisconsin received an extra bounty of $25.[32]

On Sunday, November 2nd at 8 AM the regiment marched through freshly fallen snow onto a train—filling 22 cars. They reached Chicago at 7PM and marched through the city to the Illinois Central Railroad depot. At 10 PM the train departed for Cairo, at the southern extremity of Illinois. Since there was a rumor of outlaws who might attack the train, 14 riflemen from each company were posted on the car platforms.[33] The train passed through the night largely without incident. However, coupling pins broke three times in the night, which caused considerable delay.[34]

The train arrived in Cairo on the morning of November 4th. The city, located at the confluence of the Ohio and Mississippi Rivers, was of great strategic importance. One man of the 29th Wisconsin counted twenty steamships and four gunboats on the Ohio River alone. From 3 to 4 PM the regiment boarded the "New Uncle Sam" and packed over 1000 men onto the steamship. At dusk, they departed Cairo "knowing only

Cairo 1862

Soldiers embark the New Uncle Sam at Cairo

The junction of the Ohio and Mississippi rivers looking south to "Rebeldom." The campaigns to control the rivers of the West dominated generals' strategic plans for most of the war in the "Western Theater."

that we were going south," one man wrote.[35] The officers knew their destination to be Helena, Arkansas.

On the morning November 5, the "New Uncle Sam" stopped somewhere on the Tennessee shore of the Mississippi to take on wood and to let most of the men cook a breakfast of coffee and bacon —guarded by "fifty resolute fellows with loaded rifles."[36] Yet some southern Americans did not need to be guarded against. As the "New Uncle Sam" continued south past Fort Pillow, the 29th Wisconsin passed by "five or six negroes" who were "swinging their hats and cheering lustily." The regiment cheered in reply. Barely a month before, President Lincoln had signed the Emancipation Proclamation which would go into effect on January 1, 1863. One soldier expressed his goodwill to the enslaved persons writing "Toil on, a few more days poor fellows and the 'Jubilee' will come." Others were less concerned with the well-being of the enslaved but saw ending slavery as the fastest way to end the war. Another soldier wrote home later in the week, "A general emancipation is *the* blow—one that will tell the story of peace to generations yet unborn. Let the negro take care of himself, and the planter do the same…Knock out the prop, and the structure it supports will speedily fall."[37]

Yet the sights of slavery were not the only perceptible changes for the northerners. Along the river the steamboat passed earthworks, cannons, and chimneys—all that remained of burned homes. The men were issued ammunition. One wrote, "the boys are preparing for 'secesh' showers of bullets, which are common in this latitude."[38]

On the morning of November 6th, the 29th Wisconsin finally arrived at their largely undisclosed destination: Helena, Arkansas. The small town was a major Union base on the Mississippi and was overwhelmed with tens of thousands of Union soldiers. One 29th Wisconsin man observed, "Long rows of tents dot the shore for miles." Reportedly, the army had so thoroughly raided the surrounding Arkansas

Camp of the 29th Iowa at Helena

countryside for supplies that forage parties had to travel 18 miles away to gather anything of value.[39]

After conferring with General Alvin P. Hovey, Colonel Gill ordered the regiment to the opposite side of the river in Mississippi for the regiment's campground. According to one regimental officer, Gill preferred the Mississippi side because he wanted a clear camping ground and hoped to find abundant forage opportunities. Furthermore, the large amounts of troops in Helena had made the place "very dirty."[40]

Quartermaster Samuel Baird reported that Gill had called a meeting of the company captains and the majority voted to camp in Mississippi because it was better camp site and that the troops already in Helena were "very much

General Alvin P. Hovey

demoralized." Fearing, perhaps, the camp's isolated position or the threat of disease, Baird wrote "I expect that some day not far hence, we shall be erased from the army list as a regiment."[41]

Rebel marksmen had been firing from the state of Mississippi into boats on the river and even into the Helena encampment in Arkansas. Everyday half of one of the Union regiments in Helena was shipped across the river to guard and patrol the Mississippi shore. These units reportedly suffered 16 casualties in two weeks.[42] The 29th Wisconsin was the first Union unit to permanently occupy the Mississippi side so they had the task of establishing a camp, naming it "Camp Salomon" in honor of the governor. The colonel selected four overgrown acres around a small cotton trader's cabin for the site of the camp—the only cleared area in an otherwise dense forest.[43] Within days, despite lacking tools, the Wisconsin men erected huts. Captain W. A. De La Maytr commented on the men's ingenuity and peculiar resourcefulness, "At first the hard crackers were thought to be useless, but every day they become more handy for chinking and shingles. Water won't penetrate."[44]

The next morning, November 7th, 400 men stood guard around the camp. Orders also went out for 30 volunteers from each company, about 300 men total, to head out on a foraging and scouting expedition. It is unclear where Ganske was assigned. The men on the expedition were ordered to take only their arms and canteen. Being in "the heart of rebeldom," Captain Hezekiah Dunham of Fox Lake saw that "every precaution was taken to prevent surprise" by sending out flankers on each side of the column. Early on the detachment encountered "a planter on horseback having a little negro boy on behind him." The man claimed to be a loyal Union man and produced papers ordering the protection of his property from Union foraging parties. Nonetheless, Captain Dunham commandeered the man's white horse and said, "we will look your plantation over."[45]

    At first the Wisconsinites cautiously approached the plantation and surrounded the buildings. Although the planter had asserted his loyalty to the Union, the slaves contended that a band of rebel guerillas had eaten breakfast there just that morning.[46] Dunham gave orders to "take all that could be carried away that would be of any service" adding that anything they wanted was theirs. One eyewitness wrote back to Wisconsin, "I wish it were possible to describe the scene that followed…it was almost impossible to restrain the men." The soldiers seized turkeys, chickens, ducks, and pigs and "compelled them to lie quietly." The men were forbidden to use their guns, so they grabbed stones and clubs and "drove pell mell at everything valuable." The men quickly seized horses and mules and harnessed them to confiscated wagons, carriages, and carts and loaded them bacon, corn, rope, and anything else they could get their hands on. The soldiers also took three "prisoners:" the planter, an overseer, and "a suspicious looking *stranger* who had been 'stopping there over night [sic].'" The foraging party returned to Camp Salomon in the afternoon. The rest of the regiment "gathered around to see the spoils."[47] One of the men who had remained in the camp recalled that four

The return of a foraging party

prisoners were brought in, along with eight African Americans as well as "rebel letters" and money.[48] One man wrote home, "Don't you call that a pretty good commencement for the second day in rebeldom?"[49]

The common soldiers seemed to have no idea who the planter was. However, Baird, on the regimental staff, noted that it was General James Alcorn. Alcorn ran a large plantation, practiced law, and served in the Mississippi state legislature before the war. Personally, he opposed secession and attempted to stall the vote, but nevertheless voted for it, seeing the movement's popularity and momentum. He was elected as brigadier general of state troops, but by the end of 1862 he no longer held any command. Alcorn urged the arming of slaves to resist Federal occupation to no avail. Alcorn

James L. Alcorn

33

was also a constant critic of fellow Mississippian, Confederate President Jefferson Davis.[50]

Alcorn had developed his estate, Mound Place Plantation located along the Yazoo Pass, into a profitable cotton operation.[51] The 1860 census recorded that he had 77 slaves on the eve of war.

Quartermaster Baird, like other witnesses, had also noted that Alcorn had claimed to be a Union man and had protection papers signed by a U.S. general. Yet the slaves had insisted that Alcorn was a "rank secessionist." Alcorn was a complicated man. Was the ransacking of Alcorn's home justified? Lacking local

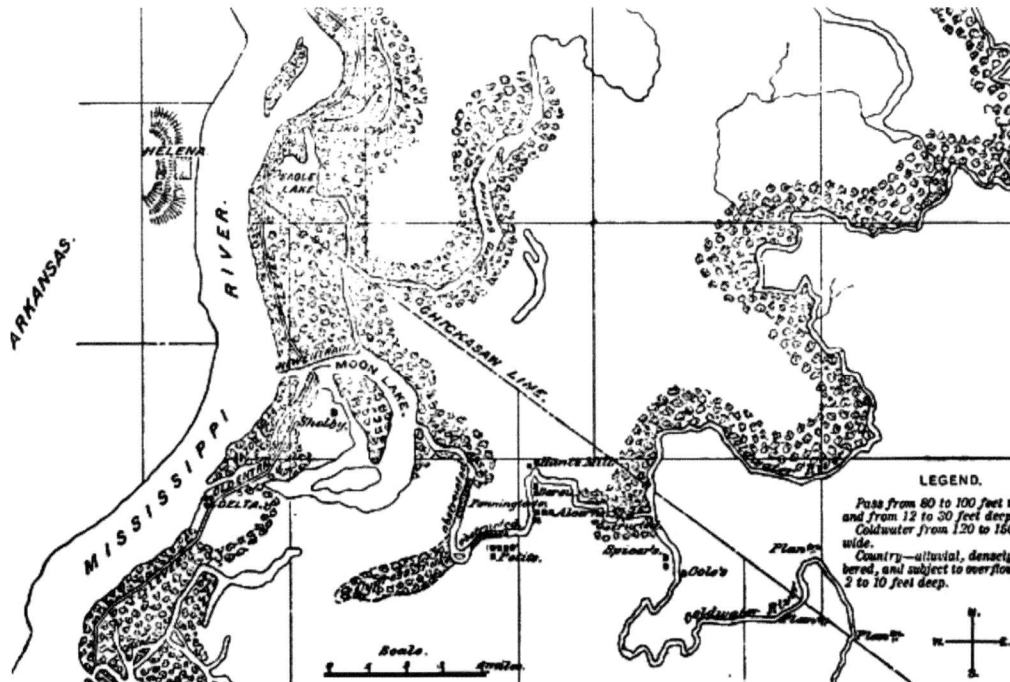

This map of the Yazoo Pass Expedition shows Helena in the top right. Camp Salomon would have been located near Eagle Lake directly across from Helena. Alcorn's plantation is just visible in the bottom center of the map.

knowledge, no one in the 29th Wisconsin seemed to care very much. When Baird composed his letter a few days later, another foraging party returned with a large load of goods from another plantation. He opined, "It looks to me a good deal like grand larceny, plain folks call it stealing." Baird noted the plight of local civilians, "No matter what are their sentiments, they are plundered by both sides."[52]

The evening of the raid on Alcorn's plantation appeared to be an ideal time for rebel retaliation. Baird reported, "Firing was heard from the pickets, the long roll was beat, and the entire regiment formed on the color line in battle array. It was dark, and the stillness was oppressive."[53] One enlisted man's account asserted that a rebel scout had briefly exchanged fire with the

On Picket in the Woods by Edwin Forbes

35

pickets before escaping without injury on either side.[54] Another man wrote that it "was nothing but a loose mule in the brush." Later that night the alarm was sounded again and the whole regiment came into battle line in three minutes. However, it was another false alarm. One man wrote, "That time I believe they killed a cow. The boys are so afraid of guerrillas that they don't wait to see what is coming before they fire."[55] With rumors of Union soldiers having recently been shot in the vicinity, the fresh 29th Wisconsin spent an uneasy first night in enemy territory.[56] Another soldier wrote, "No rebel forces are supposed to be near us, but guerillas infest the whole country…these we dread because of their cat-like stealthiness [sic] and swift maneuverings."[57]

    The men handled their fear in various ways. Baird reported,

> I went along the line to get orders from the Colonel and found the boys breathing short, but never flinched however, excepting one poor fellow who wilted like a cabbage leaf in midsummer, and took himself off to the hospital, but not being able to define his symptoms, except that he felt *'kind o' terribly all over.'* The surgeon sent him back faster than he came.[58]

Although not one man had been shot by Confederate bullets, the 29th Wisconsin's regimental hospital was rapidly filling up. Within days of arriving in Mississippi

15 to 20 sick men were hospitalized in a sympathetic local's log cabin.

Since Camp Salomon was one of the only Union positions on the Mississippi side of the river, it became the refuge of countless escaped slaves. Captain W. A. De La Matyr of company K reported, "Contrabands are flocking in on every side, and exhibit no little tact in answering the many questions asked them." De La Matyr unsympathetically noted that some former slaves wanted to work, but the majority would rather enjoy their new-found freedom and "sit down by the river and sun themselves." He added, "There are hundreds of acres of cotton near here, but the planters have skedaddled."[59]

Coming into the Lines by Edwin Forbes.

White River Expedition

On November 15th the 29th Wisconsin was ordered to supply a hand-picked 400-man contingent for an expedition under the command of General Hovey. This large operation would involve thousands of other troops, including cavalry and artillery [60] August Ganske of company H was among them.[61] The enlisted men were ordered to take three days rations, but were left ignorant of their destination. On the 16th The 29th Wisconsin embarked on board the *Decatur* and *Tecumseh,* two of fourteen transports, guarded by the Gunboat *Carondelet.*

The USS Carondelet participated in the capture of Fort Henry and Fort Donelson and many other operations including engaging in battle with the ironclad CSS Arkansas.

One participant from the 29th described the scene in Helena:

> The bustle of preparation—the blowing of the steam whistles—the clatter of arms—the mingled curses of mule drivers—cavalrymen—sailors—soldirs [sic] and officials, were in sad contrast with the quiet and the sweetly chiming church bells of a thousand northern cities and villages.[62]

The fleet cautiously steamed south through enemy territory, fearful not only of enemy attack, but of natural obstacles in the low-flowing Mississippi River. Nonetheless the *Decatur* got stuck on a sandbar and took considerable effort to make progress. Furthermore, one man of company D of the 29th Wisconsin was shot in the back by a rebel guerilla while carrying wood back to his steamboat. Adding insult to injury, one of the ship

The Union's large "brown water navy" enabled the army to attack deep into the Confederacy along major waterways.

captains accidently shot and wounded himself with his own revolver.[63] Despite the mishaps, after two days the fleet anchored at the mouth of the White River and sent out the cavalry to reconnoiter. Only at that point did the enlisted men perceive the expedition's goal: they were to steam up the White River for about 12 miles, then disembark and march the remaining three miles to Fort Hindman at Arkansas Post and "reduce" its fortifications.[64]

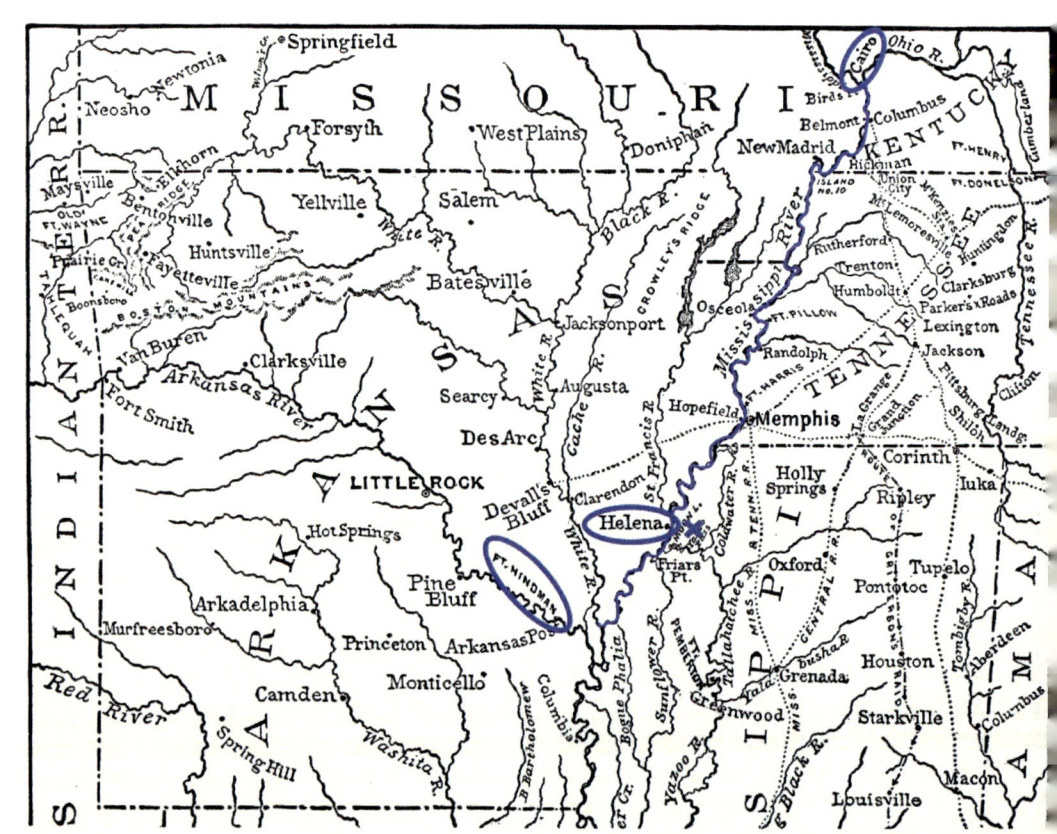

The Operations of the 29th Wisconsin in November 1862. The "X" marks the general location of Camp Salomon.

The Union flotilla attempted to lighten the boats' loads and ascend the White River, but the low water prevented any progress. November 19th saw much of the army waiting at the mouth of the White River, waiting for the cavalry to return, while a few foraging parties returned with mules, cattle, pigs, and poultry. One enlisted man wrote, "The riverbank presents the appearance of a wholesale slaughter yard." He added,

> These foraging parties generally go to extremes and do things perfectly disgraceful. Here we learn a widow woman has had her house burned and yonder a poor old negro is robbed of all he possessed…in vain they plead.

The man believed he represented sizable part of the army that believed in sharp distinctions between confiscating rebel property and "indiscriminate wholesale stealing." He believed that "reckless and inefficient commanders" were primarily to blame.[65] Another man lamented,

> we burned a house, occupied by a defenceless [sic] woman and two children…beside pillaging the country for miles each way, taking every thing we could find whether we wanted it or not. The negroes themselves who are so generally on our side learned horrible things of the yankees [sic], and when a servile insurrection is raised in our favor it will not be in that section of the South…If our army was under the discipline it ought to be under, no such tales would be related at the firesides of Southern homes as will be

related in times to come. I am as much in favor as anybody of living upon the enemy, but the greatest villain should have a limit to his punishment.[66]

The evening of November 19th the cavalry returned. Their report was not encouraging. The Confederates at Fort Hindman were aware of the Union expedition sent against them. Furthermore, they had improved their fortifications. The report circulated that they had 40 pieces of artillery and supposedly 8 or 10 thousand troops. It was concluded that without more troops and heavy artillery, the expedition could not succeed. As the men re-embarked onto the steamboats Mathias Lukas of company I of the 29th Wisconsin fell overboard and drowned. The rest of the expedition arrived in Helena on November 22nd "having accomplished *nothing*" one man wrote.[67]

Yet *something* happened to August Ganske. He got sick.

Decades later, Ganske would report that poor shelter, wet weather, "hard service" and bad water and food made him sick with diarrhea. Although in modern times diarrhea is at worst an unpleasant inconvenience, in the 19th century it was often fatal. At the same time, he contracted a fever, possibly typhus, which caused him severe pain on his left side and back.

The rainy winter and poor shelter at Camp Salomon likely did not help Ganske's condition. Captain Thomas Mott from Watertown, Wisconsin wrote, "We have suffered more from rain than cold, owing to the poorness of our tents. They are very scanty...The men have now built log huts, which they cover with them, and have made themselves quite comfortable. By means of a small stick and mud chimney they keep a fire and mange to keep tolerably dry."[68]

Soldier's winter quarters were improvised and non-standard.

The Angel of Wisconsin

One December 20, 1862 one man wrote of Ganske, "We regret to say that three of four of [the men from Trenton] are unfit for duty…Some of them we fear will never be fit for duty again, but at present it seems impossible for any to obtain a discharge. How unreasonable and cruel to keep men here to die, after being well satisfied they can be of no earthly use to the service." He added that Surgeon Spalding excused 50 to 75 men a day from duty. Four men had died within the last two weeks. Yet the man did not blame the medical staff saying, "The care and attention bestowed upon the sick in the Hospital is of the most faithful character. An experience of nearly two weeks enables us to know whereof we speak. Let our friends at home rest assured that *all* that can be, is done for the comfort and recovery of the sick."[69] Lieutenant Darius S. Gibbs of company B in the 29th Wisconsin wrote that the regimental Surgeon, William Spalding, assisted by his wife, "has his hands full, but manages his department well."[70] Another soldier wrote of Mrs. Spalding's "kind attentions" to him when he was sick. Another man added, "The sunny face of Mrs. L. P. Harvey made the sick ones happy."

Cordelia Adelaide Harvey was no stranger to suffering. Her husband, Louis Harvey, was elected governor of Wisconsin in 1861 yet tragically drowned seventy-three days later having fallen off a boat while visiting Wisconsin troops in the South. In September 1862, as the 29th Wisconsin was being formed, Governor Salomon appointed Mrs. Harvey as a "sanitary agent" who would visit sick Wisconsin soldiers in hospitals and look after their welfare.[71]

Harvey was appalled by conditions in the hospitals. She saw many young men die—she was convinced unnecessarily. She wrote of the sick,

> But if, as was too frequently the case, he was sent to convalescent camps, in a few weeks he was returned to the hospital, and again to camp and thus continued to vibrate between camp and hospital until hope and life were gone. This was the fate of thousands.

She believed that sick men needed furloughs so they could be released from the deadly hospitals and recover in the comfort of their homes.[72] While she may have incorrectly assumed

Cordelia A. P. Harvey

that northern men would recover in a northern climate, the sick would almost certainly have fared better away from unsanitary conditions and the destructive medical practices of the surgeons.

As she dined on a steamer on the way to Helena, she overheard an officer, the medical director at Helena, state that it was cheaper to keep soldiers in hospitals than to furlough them. This sentiment was shared by General Henry Halleck, commander of the Western Theatre. When Harvey arrived at Helena, Harvey recalled "I found over two thousand graves of Northerners. Two-thirds of these men might have been saved, could they have been sent north." When she asked the surgeon of the general hospital why he did not furlough men from his overflowing hospitals, he replied that had filled out hundreds of furlough certificates, but the medical director denied them all and ordered them back to the hospital. The surgeon told Harvey, "many of them never returned, for, brokenhearted, they have lain down by the roadside and died."[73]

Seeing firsthand the suffering of Ganske and many others compelled Harvey to embark on reform campaign. She would meet with General Ulysses S. Grant, Secretary of War Edwin Stanton, and even Abraham Lincoln. Many months after her visit to

Helena, Harvey's efforts were rewarded. Lincoln authorized her to establish hospitals in Wisconsin to alleviate the suffering of the sick and wounded.[74]

On December 23rd the 29th Wisconsin was ordered to break up camp and join the main body of troops in Helena. The regiment was relocated to a hill overlooking Helena, about a mile from the Mississippi River. Unfortunately, the tents and baggage did not arrive until the next day. One man wrote, "No alternative but to lie down on the ground without supper (save a little hard tack) and wait for morning." Concerning men like Ganske, he added, "The sick were moved first, and were made as comfortable as possible, yet we fear more of our brave boys *must die*." The very next day, Christmas Eve, the regiment was ordered to report to General Gorman for an expedition to Friar's Point. However, Ganske and the other very sick men would be left behind in horrible Helena.

> The few we cannot take are moved down to another tent. As they are carried by on a stretcher, we gather around to say good bye. We look upon that pallid check and sunken eye—it is for the last time brave boy, and then to die alone too—we turn away to weep.[75]

Ganske was placed in the General Hospital in Helena, where the odds were against his survival.

Samuel Baird wrote that the locals pronounced Helena as "Hell-no" but that, "it ought to be hell-yes."

Another man in the 29th Wisconsin wrote, "if you wish to perfect an idea how a town can look without the presence of God, visit Helena and you will have it."[76] Historian Rhonda M. Kohl has described Northern-occupied Helena as "one of the most insalubrious locations in the Union."

Through the lens of modern medical knowledge, Kohl examined the treatment of dysentery and other diseases in Helena from July 1862 to January 1863, incidentally, covering the same time and cause of Ganske's hospitalization. Kohl wrote that many

One of Helena's filthy streets during the Civil War

soldiers died, "because of the lack of understanding by medical authorities of the etiological cause of the disease, the relationship among sanitation, the environment and health, and the types of drugs used." An ignorance of germ theory meant that doctors incorrectly diagnosed both the cause and the cure of diseases. A similarity of symptoms between diseases like malaria, typhus and typhoid caused doctors to misdiagnose their patients' diseases entirely.[77]

    This caused many soldiers to fear the hospital and the regimental surgeons' treatments. Many viewed the hospital as a death sentence and preferred home remedy among the tents of their comrades—in one instance a soldier preferred the horse doctor over the surgeon.

    Ganske's diagnosis, "chronic diarrhea," along with other intestinal disease, caused more sickness and death than any other kind of disease in the Civil War. Ganske's belief that "bad" food and water led to his illness was likely correct, but for the wrong reasons. Dysentery is caused by a parasite called Entamoeba histolytica and is often spread by uncooked food contaminated with feces from infected people. However, flies and cockroaches also spread the disease. While mild cases last from four to eight days, severe cases last for six weeks or longer. Dehydration would often end in death. Survivors could retain the parasites for years.[78]

However Civil War surgeons were ignorant of parasites and believed that symptoms of diarrhea meant that the patient was not sweating enough, a result, they believed, of eating spoiled meat and underripe fruit or drinking "impure" water. To purify the diseased intestinal tract, doctors would apply treatments like the "Blue Pill," a mercury purgative mixed with chalk. This and other mercury-based medicine, caused more harm than good. Mercury, a poison, causes mental confusion, nervous system damage, gastrointestinal irritation, nausea and vomiting, kidney damage, liver damage, convulsions and tremors, and diarrhea—the very symptom the "medicine" was meant to treat. Furthermore, opium was often prescribed to relieve pain, albeit only administered once after the initial purge. Other common medicines, like turpentine, were equally harmful to the patients. [79] In November, when Ganske was first hospitalized, 1,800 men were hospitalized for intestinal diseases in Helena. By the time he was sent to the General Hospital at Jefferson Barracks on January 2, 1863, Helena was overflowing with over 3,000 cases of intestinal disease. The

The Hospital at Jefferson Barracks, St. Louis, Missouri

combined toll of disease on the Army of the Southwest at Helena meant that 35 percent of the army was unavailable for duty from November 1862 through January 1863.[80]

On January 30, 1863, the Jefferson Barracks commander discharged Ganske after the hospital surgeon certified that he had been unfit for duty for two months due to "chronic spinal meningitis, incipient arthritis, and general prostration." Ganske received a "Certificate of Disability for Discharge," likely so he could return home without being stopped as a deserter and so he could have written testimony that he was not dishonorably discharged. Ganske was far from alone, during the war 223, 535 soldiers were given disability discharges from the Union army.[81]

Ganske would suffer from severe diarrhea for a whole year after his discharge from the army.

Never Forgotten

Despite lingering health issues Ganske was determined to make the most of his life. On October 18, 1863 he married Margaret Anna Krause of Oak Grove. She was born in Massachusetts to John and Anna Kraus, immigrants from Wuerttemberg. The couple had seven children: Lucellia, William, Anna, August, John, Albert, and Charles.

Yet Ganske never fully recovered from his Civil War disability. In 1886 he received a pension for four dollars a month. In August 1887 he re-applied for a pension for six dollars a month and stated that he continued to suffer "chronic diarrhea, disease of liver and back," claiming they were all the results of the fevers he suffered while sick in the army. Ganske stated that six to eight times a year he suffered from attacks of the "disease," each episode lasting several days. His medical examination found Ganske to be in "pretty good health." The surgeon recommended a "1/2 rating for the disability caused by chronic diarrhea." The slow workings of bureaucracy continued Ganske's pension process well into 1888. In May Ganske signed a statement of facts and requested the testimony of his long-time friends and neighbors, such as Betsy Whiting,

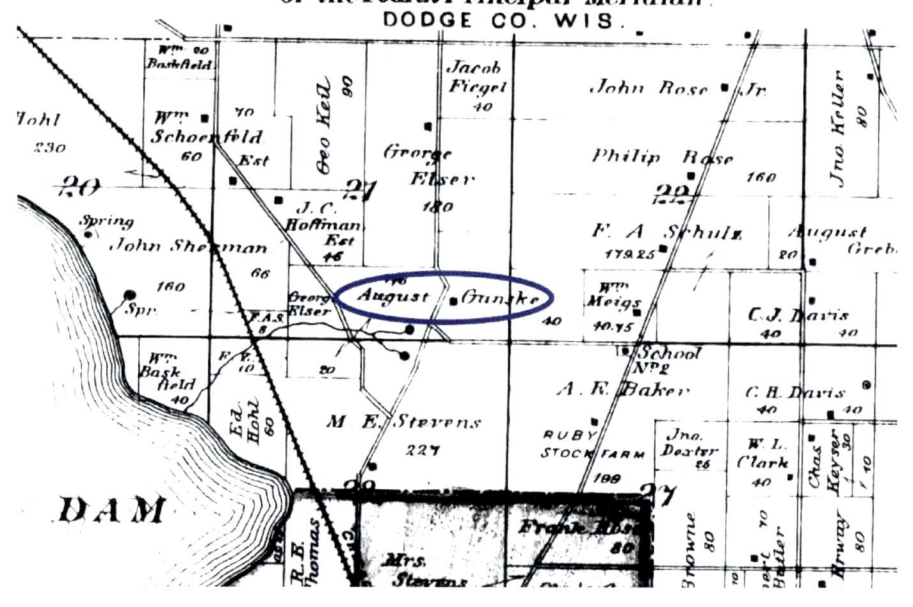

Ganske owned a 146-acre farm directly north of Beaver Dam

Ganske visited Dr. Spalding in Watertown, the 29th Wisconsin's surgeon during Ganske's illness hoping to get him to sign the affidavit, but Spalding said that he could not recall Ganske after 25 years and that all his record books had been sent to Washington D.C., leaving him no records to reference. Ganske's claim for liver disease and back pain was rejected in November 1888, but his he was approved for a pension of six dollars a month for his chronic diarrhea.

Ganske did not see all aspects of his military service and suffering as a negative experience that deserved compensation. He was an active member of the Dodge County Veterans Association and attended reunions of the 29th Wisconsin.

In 1900 Margaret Anna Ganske died. The next year August Ganske transferred his farm of 80 acres to his eldest son William for one dollar and purchased two lots in Beaver Dam for $3,000. In 1903 August Ganske married Ida Weidman. In 1905 Ganske appealed for a larger pension, eight dollars a month, claiming that his disability incapacitated him from doing manual labor on his farm. Following an act of Congress passed in 1907 for all veterans, Ganske applied again in October 1908 for an additional 15 dollars a month. Meanwhile, Ida had died in January 1908. Nine months later Ganske remarried for a third time to Mary Gilmore, a 38-year-old farmer's daughter from Randolph.

On March 6, 1911 August Ganske died in Beaver Dam. He is buried in the city cemetery. His obituary concluded, "Mr. Ganske was an enterprising and successful farmer, a veteran of the Civil War, a good citizen, and a humble Christian. He was beloved in his family and greatly respected by all who knew him."

Selected Bibliography

Unpublished Sources
The August Ganske file at the National Archives

Quiner's Scrapbooks at the Wisconsin Historical Society

Published Sources
Dougherty, Kevin J. 2010. *Encyclopedia of the Confederacy.* San Diego: Thunder Bay Press.

Harvey, Cordelia A. P. 1918. "A Wisconsin Woman's Picture of President Lincoln." *Wisconsin Magazine of History*, March: 233-255.

Klement, Frank L. 2001. *Wisconsin in the Civil War.* Madison: State Historical Society of Wisconsin.

Kohl, Rhonda M. 2004. ""This Godforsaken Town": Death and Disease at Helena, Arkansas, 1862-63." *Civil War History*, June: 109-144.

Larson, Ronald Paul. 2017. *Wisconsin and the Civil War.* Charleston: The History Press.

Miller, Mary Carol. 2010. *Lost Mansions of Mississippi.* University Press of Mississippi.

Whipple, Henry P. 1906. *The Diary of a Private Soldier.* Waterloo, Wisconsin.

Endnotes.

[1] Kohl, Rhonda M. 2004. ""This Godforsaken Town": Death and Disease at Helena, Arkansas, 1862-63." *Civil War History*, June: 109-144.

[2] Grace Ganske Vachon article "The Man of Good." Unknown publication and date. The author happens to share Ganske's birthday.

[3] Phelps, Benjamin, *Friedrich Wyneken: Untiring Lutheran of the American West.* Unpublished manuscript.

[4] Vachon.

[5] Larson, Ronald Paul. 2017. *Wisconsin and the Civil War.* Charleston: The History Press. 16.

[6] Larson, 21.

[7] Larson, 106-108.

[8] Larson, 108-109.

[9] *Fox Lake Gazette,* August 20, 1862.

[10] *Fox Lake Gazette*, August 20, 1862, 4. Trenton furiously complained that Beaver Dam had counted men from Trenton on their quota. $100 in 1862 is worth over $2,500 in 2020.

[11] *Fox Lake Gazette*, August 27, 1862, 4.

[12] Vachon.

[13] Whipple, Henry P. 1906. *The Diary of a Private Soldier.* Waterloo, Wisconsin. 1.

[14] Quiner Scrapbooks: Correspondence of the Wisconsin Volunteers, 1861-1865, Volume 7.3. Wisconsin Historical Society collection.

[15] *Fox Lake Gazette*, October 1, 1862, 1.

[16] Quiner, Volume 7. 3.

[17] For example, see *Fox Lake Gazette* September 10, 1862, 4.

[18] Quiner, Volume 6. 319.

[19] Quiner, Volume 6. 322.

[20] Quiner, Volume 7. 5.

[21] Emilie Quiner's Diary, 1861-1863, 54. Wisconsin Historical Society collection.

[22] Quiner, Volume 7. 3.

[23] Quiner, Volume 7. 3.

[24] Quiner, Volume 6. 322.

[25] Quiner, Volume 7. 2.

[26] Quiner, Volume 7. 5.

[27] Quiner, Volume 7. 4.

[28] Quiner, Volume 7. 4.

[29] Quiner, Volume 7. 5.

[30] Quiner, Volume 7. 4. Original italics.
[31] Quiner, Volume 7. 4.
[32] Quiner, Volume 7. 5.
[33] Quiner, Volume 6. 325.
[34] Quiner, Volume 6. 328.
[35] Quiner, Volume 6. 325. Another man wrote about seeing several Confederate prisoners about to be sent south for a prisoner exchange. The 29th Wisconsin man talked with one of the POWs who claimed to have once lived in Beaver Dam, Wisconsin. The writer noted, "nothing would afford him greater gratification than to cut some his old neighbors throats."
[36] Quiner, Volume 6. 325. Another account says 100 men.
[37] Quiner, Volume 6. 326.
[38] Quiner, Volume 6. 326.
[39] Quiner, Volume 6. 327.
[40] Quiner, Volume 6. 328.
[41] Quiner, Volume 6. 329.
[42] Quiner, Volume 6. 327.
[43] Quiner, Volume 6. Another soldier wrote that they called the landing "Solomon's Landing" and the camp "Camp Gill."
[44] Quiner, Volume 6. 331.
[45] Quiner, Volume 6. According to the *Roster of Wisconsin Volunteers, War of the Rebellion, 1861-1865*, Volume I, Dunham was dishonorably discharged on May 11, 1863 for undisclosed reasons.
[46] Quiner, Volume 6. 328.
[47] Quiner, Volume 6. 327
[48] Quiner, Volume 6. 326. This account says, "six mules and eights[sic] niggers were taken." The verbiage indicates that the writer saw these eight people as part of the spoils of war, rather than freed individuals. However, at the time, racial slurs were much more common and liberated slaves were referred to as "contraband." Before the Emancipation Proclamation, Union officers referred to escaped slaves as confiscated enemy military resources to justify not returning them to slavery according to the Fugitive Slave Act. In 1855, the Wisconsin Supreme Court became the only state high court to declare the Fugitive Slave Act unconstitutional.
[49] Quiner, Volume 6. 328.
[50] Dougherty, Kevin J. 2010. *Encyclopedia of the Confederacy.* San Diego: Thunder Bay Press. 11. The Mississippi Archives have the letters and papers of James L. Alcorn, including his diary in which he records his plantation being raided. Following the raid on his plantation, Alcorn speculated in the cotton black market. He was later a Republican governor of Mississippi and later a U.S. senator.

[51] Miller, Mary Carol. 2010. *Lost Mansions of Mississippi.* University Press of Mississippi. 115.

[52] Quiner, Volume 6. 329.
[53] Quiner, Volume 6. 329.
[54] Quiner, Volume 6. 326.
[55] Quiner, Volume 6. 328. Another man wrote, "A straw cow advanced upon the sleepless picket, and failing to give the countersign as commanded, was unceremoniously shot down, a warning to all secession cows. This is the first blood shed by the 29th." Quiner, Volume 6. 331.
[56] Quiner, Volume 6. 326.
[57] Quiner, Volume 6. 328
[58] Quiner, Volume 6. 329.
[59] Quiner, Volume 6. 331.
[60] Quiner, Volume, 6. 331. One account says 15,000 another suggests 9,000 troops were involved.
[61] Ganske file. One 29th Wisconsin officer wrote that the men were carefully selected.
[62] Quiner, Volume 6. 332.
[63] Quiner, Volume 6. 333.
[64] Quiner, Volume 6. 332.
[65] Quiner, Volume 6. 332.
[66] Quiner, Volume 6. 334. Another man from the 29th Wisconsin wrote home in December that statements about "burning dwellings, ravishing women, and ruthlessly destroying property to be false, and a slander upon as orderly and well behaved a body of troops as ever went to war." 336.
[67] Quiner, Volume 6. 332, 333, 334. Also spelled Mathias Lokas, Lakes and Lacas.
[68] Quiner, Volume 6. 335. Another man later wrote on December 20, 1862 that the regiment finally received army issue "wedge tents." The cabins were built in rows with streets about 20 feet wide, the gable end to the street. The cabins were about seven by ten feet and about five feet high with the old shelter tents as coverings. Each cabin accommodated a squad of four to six men who lived and cooked together. Each squad had one frying pan, coffee pot, mess pan, and camp kettle. Each man had his own plate, cup, spoon, knife, and fork.
[69] Quiner, Volume 6. 336.
[70] Quiner, Volume 6. 334.
[71] Klement, Frank L. 2001. *Wisconsin in the Civil War.* Madison: State Historical Society of Wisconsin. 115.
[72] Harvey, Cordelia A. P. 1918. "A Wisconsin Woman's Picture of

President Lincoln." *Wisconsin Magazine of History*, March: 233-255. 236.
[73] Harvey, 237.
[74] Klement, 116.
[75] Quiner, Volume 6. 336.
[76] Quiner, Volume 6. 330.
[77] Kohl, 111.
[78] Kohl, 120.
[79] Kohl, 120-22.
[80] Kohl, 143.
[81] Kohl, 112.

Made in the USA
Columbia, SC
11 December 2020